York *Courses* are produced by Simon Stanley and John Young. All courses (audio tapes or CDs with notes or booklets) are designed for groups and individuals. They involve distinguished contributors from a wide range of churches and traditions. This makes the material ideal for ecumenical use.

In addition, York *Courses* has produced a number of Topic Tapes.

We have also published a series of seven booklets on key topics in 'The Archbishop's School' series. These attractive but inexpensive booklets are commissioned  ʳchbishop of York.

ils of all our products are in the centre pages ooklet.

 *Courses* have gathered yet er fine team for yet another stimulating course ... No wonder tens of thousands of people – from Britain and overseas – use these ecumenical courses year on year.

\+ ⌐⌐⌐ Eᴸᴺ;

Archbishop of York from 1995-2005

© York *Courses:* December 2004

OUR WARM THANKS to Mark Comer of The Max Design & Print co. for his invaluable help and expertise. Sincere thanks also to Yolande Clarke, Carrie Geddes and Linda Norman for proof reading, to Barbara Thompson who prepared the manuscript for printing and to Jerry Ibbotson and his team at Media Mill for editing the audio tape/CD.

PHOTOS: Sincere thanks to Colin Paterson for the front cover and page 5. Warm thanks to the UNITED BIBLE SOCIETIES for page 20 (children from Colombia; photo by Larry Jerden). The photo of Dr David Hope (above) is by John Angerson.

BETTER together?

A course on relationships in five parts

Written by
David Gamble
and John Young

YORK
COURSES

SUGGESTIONS FOR GROUP LEADERS

1 THE ROOM — Discourage people from sitting outside or behind the main circle – all need to be equally involved.

2. HOSPITALITY — Tea or coffee on arrival can be helpful at the first meeting. Perhaps at the end too, to encourage people to talk informally. Some groups might be more ambitious, taking it in turns to bring a dessert to start the evening (even in Lent, hospitality is OK!) with coffee at the end.

3. THE START — If group members do not know each other well, some kind of 'icebreaker' might be helpful. You might invite people to share something quite secular (where they grew up, holidays, hobbies, significant object, etc.) or something more 'spiritual' (one thing I like and one thing I dislike about my church/denomination). Place a time limit on this exercise.

4. PREPARING THE GROUP — Take the group into your confidence, e.g. 'I've never done this before', or 'I've led lots of groups and each one has contained surprises'. Sharing vulnerability is designed to encourage all members to see the success of the group as their responsibility. Encourage those who know that they talk easily to ration their contributions. You might introduce a fun element by producing a bell which all must obey instantly. Encourage the reticent to speak at least once or twice – however briefly. Explain that there are no 'right' answers and that among friends it is fine to say things that you are not sure about – to express half-formed ideas. But, of course, if individuals choose to say nothing, that is all right too.

5. THE MATERIAL — Encourage members to read next week's chapter before the meeting, if possible. There is no need to consider all the questions. A lively exchange of views is what matters, so be selective. If you wish to spread a session over two or more meetings, that's fine.

You might decide to replay all or part of the audio tape/CD – the closing reflection for example – at the end.

For some questions you might start with a few minutes' silence to make jottings. Or you might ask members to talk in sub-groups of two or three, before sharing with the whole group.

6. PREPARATION — Decide beforehand whether to distribute (or ask people to bring) paper, pencils, hymn books, etc. If possible, ask people in advance to read a Bible passage or lead in prayer, so that they can prepare.

7. TIMING — Try to start on time and make sure you stick fairly closely to your stated finishing time.

TRANSCRIPT

A word-by-word TRANSCRIPT of the audio tape/CD is available. GROUP LEADERS in particular may find this helpful in their preparation, whilst other group members may wish to have a transcript for easy reference. (See centre pages of this booklet.)

SESSION 1
FAMILY RELATIONSHIPS

BETTER together?

A course on relationships in five parts

YORK COURSES

Written by David Gamble and John Young

A time of change

We are living at a time of rapid change in family life, when many talk of the 'decline of the traditional family'. Compared with most of the twentieth century:

- fewer people in Britain get married nowadays
- people often marry at a later age and have fewer, if any, children
- more unmarried couples live together, though 'common law marriage' has no legal status
- same-sex couples live together openly and sometimes care for children
- more (but not most) marriages end in divorce
- more children are born outside marriage than in the recent past
- there are more teenage pregnancies and sexually transmitted diseases are widespread
- more children are being raised by a single parent
- fathers are playing a greater role in rearing children though women – including working mothers – continue to provide most child care.

Not all changes in family life are seen by everyone as bad news. What some bemoan as signs of decline, others celebrate as rich diversity. Nuclear families; step – or 'blended' – families; three or four generation families; adoption; same-sex relationships; families of choice ... these varied arrangements are found on every street and in every school. It was a positive view of diversity that led those preparing a 1995 Church of England report to call it *Something to Celebrate*.

Some people, especially those not living in 'traditional' family settings, may not see churches as welcoming or understanding. They may feel excluded from church because of their chosen lifestyle. Their perception may well be mistaken, of course. They would be surprised to learn that some people who carry responsibility in the church down the road are themselves divorced or separated or in an abusive relationship or with out-of-control children. The church isn't crammed with people who live model lives. It's there for people who need all the help they can get – and who see the gospel as a priceless resource for living in the twenty-first century.

The Bible and family life

How does experience of family life in the twenty-first century relate to the Bible and Christian tradition? The

A survey carried out in 2002 for the report, *Just a piece of paper? Marriage and cohabitation*, found that 59% of respondents viewed marriage as the best kind of relationship.

2

Bible is often quoted in support of 'traditional family life'. While Jesus didn't marry, he did give marriage his blessing by attending a wedding at Cana in Galilee (John 2). He also spoke of the community of disciples as 'family' and on one occasion he told his followers to hate their parents!* His own family (the 'holy family') has been portrayed in idealistic terms. But when the Bible tells stories of family life they are often messy, far from ideal and much closer to the TV soaps than we might expect!

The Bible's first story of family life (Genesis 4) is about Cain and Abel. This is sibling rivalry at its most extreme (wiping out 25 per cent of the world's population at a stroke!). Rivalry within families is a recurring theme: Jacob and Esau; Joseph and his older brothers; the prodigal son and his older brother. Biblical characters did not all have idyllic faithful relationships either, as the story of David and Bathsheba shows (2 Samuel 11).

In other words, the Bible does four things:

- it sets out an ideal. Families should be marked by love, faithfulness, forgiveness, discipline and clear boundaries
- it describes real people in the real world as they struggle to make family life work. As always, it is realistic about failure while promising the possibility of redemption
- it offers forgiveness, a new start and God's help when they – and we – fail
- it challenges us to radical discipleship which will (for some) involve celibacy or placing the demands of God's kingdom above family ties.

The Church and family life

How do churches support people in their relationships? Do they offer realistic support – helping us to build strong families which are able to deal with difficult moments and stages? Do they help us to give and receive forgiveness and healing? Do they help us to find hope for the future when relationships break down?

Perhaps we should ask what we mean when we look to 'the Church' to provide this support. *We are the Church!* So it must be a question of mutual support and encouragement.

---

*This difficult aspect of Jesus' teaching is considered in the course *Tough Talk* (see coloured centre pages of this booklet).

Even though fewer people in Britain attend church today, many people still involve their local church at significant times. Weddings, baptisms and funerals continue to be key points of contact. Many churches have put new energy into marriage preparation. This includes preparing for the wedding service, of course. But it also involves a wider consideration of relationships within marriage, family and community.

Such preparation goes far beyond a cosy chat with the minister. It involves gathering a group of lay people with experience of money-management, sexual relations, the advent of a baby, and marital breakdown – as well as rock-solid long-lasting relationships. In some areas churches work together in providing high quality courses.

Good marriage preparation also shows that it can be helpful to discuss the husband/wife relationship in the presence of a third party. Marriage isn't simply a private affair. It affects others and can be supported by others. Churches can offer support well beyond the wedding itself. Some provide parenting groups, toddler groups, marriage and relationship counselling, divorce recovery workshops ...

How does all this relate to worship? Does our church life and worship offer space for people to bring their deep pains to God and find hope and healing? Or is church life sometimes a *threat* to our family life – making heavy demands on time and energy? Do we see Christian discipleship in terms of serving the church or can we in some way serve God in and through our relationships? If not, why do we make such huge promises in marriage and baptism?

The single person

When we were considering possible titles for this course, we settled on *Better Together*. But when a friend saw the title she pointed out that this has two problems.

First, some people are better apart! They simply can't get along together and are *not* 'better together'. Second, there are a great many single people out there. Indeed, in Britain today more people are living on their own than ever before. Of course, single people belong to a local community, with its clubs, groups and networks. On balance, however, we decided to add a question mark to the title – hence *Better Together?* Were we right?

Conclusion

Some of the questions we face today may not have the clear and fixed answers we used to take for granted. We may find some aspects of modern society difficult, confusing and painful. But we have a lot to offer from our Christian experience and understanding – not as 'experts', but as human beings who experience the same joys and pains in our relationships as everyone else. We have much to learn from one another. By committing ourselves to discovering how to build stronger human relationships, we can also deepen our understanding of our relationship with God and the meaning of words like *trust, forgiveness, reconciliation* and *love*.

Grandparents play a vital role in many families

QUESTIONS FOR GROUPS

Please read page 1 (especially paragraphs 4 and 5) before starting your discussion. Some groups will not have time to consider more than a few questions. That is fine; this is not an obstacle course!

SUGGESTED BIBLE READING: 2 Timothy 1.3-5

1. Raise any points from this booklet or the audio tape/CD with which you strongly agree or disagree.

2. Compare and contrast family life today with family life in your childhood. In what ways is it different and in what ways is it better or worse?

3. How has the Church supported and strengthened your family and other close relationships? Are there ways in which your involvement in church life has made things harder? (*Suggestion:* re-read the third and fourth paragraphs on page 4 before tackling this.)

4. Invite single people in your group to give their experiences of being included or feeling excluded. Then invite those with partners and/or families to respond to this.

5. Have you experienced something within your family life that was less than you had hoped for, but turned out to be a source of joy?

6. (a) How do churches known to you help to prepare people for marriage, bereavement or baptism?

   (b) Do you feel that the ideas for marriage preparation sketched in this chapter might be helpful? For example, in some areas churches working together organise a marriage preparation morning for several couples at once. In your view is this idea worth exploring?

7. Group members are invited to share their experiences of:

   (a) good times in family life e.g. birth, holidays, happy stability

   (b) dark times e.g. illness, bereavement, breakdown of relationships.

   At such times, how important was your faith in God and membership of a church?

8. What place do animals play in the lives of families or single people known to you, including (perhaps) your own?

9. **Read Matthew 12.46-50.** Does this suggest that the way of Jesus threatens family life? Or does it in some way transcend it?

10. **Read Ephesians 5.22-6.4.** How can we relate Bible teaching about family life to modern Britain e.g. 'wives obey your husbands'? Does that simply reflect first-century culture or should it apply today?

Closing meditation:

Read Colossians 3.12-14.

In silence pray for members of your family or neighbourhood, especially those struggling with tough decisions or situations. Then say the Lord's Prayer together.

SESSION 2

RELATIONSHIPS WITHIN THE CHURCH

In the Middle Ages, many priests were un-officially 'married' ... impecunious clergy with a household of children, presiding over a half-coherent liturgy on Sundays ... as they worked their farmland for the rest of the week, were common all over Europe'.

Professor Eamon Duffy

Sad news ...

Chloe was a mature student who wanted to reconnect with the church. She asked her college chaplain for advice and he gave her the name of a local church known to be very friendly.

When Chloe spoke to the chaplain again a few weeks later, she was almost in tears. She explained that after the Sunday service she felt frozen out. The members were indeed very friendly, but their relationships were cosy and inward-looking. They would not take time and trouble to welcome the stranger.

... and glad news

Tony – a teenager – took courage and attended his local church. He was rather bored and decided he would leave and not come back. As he headed for the exit after the service he was greeted by David, who invited Tony to the youth club. That wasn't easy for David. He had his own friends and he really wanted to meet them as he usually did. But he gave time and a welcome to Tony. The story has an interesting ending. David went on to become a lay preacher and Tony is now an archdeacon!

Images of 'Church'

In the Bible and later Christian tradition, various terms are used to describe the Church. Different models emphasise different understandings of the relationship between Christ and his Church, or between church members or between the Church and the world. Some images depict the church as a family. Other pictures emphasise different aspects: God's living temple; a royal priesthood; the bride of Christ ...

'The grace of the Lord Jesus Christ, the love of God and the fellowship of the Holy Spirit be with all of you' (2 Corinthians 13.14). Paul's famous prayer for the Christians in Corinth is used almost as often as the Lord's Prayer. Perhaps 'fellowship' is a good word to describe relationships within the church. But what does it mean?

Fellowship is different from friendship, though there is a clear overlap. For friendship to flourish there is usually a shared interest and/or compatibility of personalities. For Christian fellowship to flourish there simply needs to be a shared faith and a recognition that – however little else we might have in common – we are brothers and sisters within the Christian family.

The Body of Christ

One of the best-known images of the Church in the New Testament is that of the Body of Christ

(1 Corinthians 12.12-31; Ephesians 4.1-7). This picture emphasises the truth that all members depend on one another and need each other. No one member is more important or more necessary than another. All bring their different gifts to make up one body 'for the common good'.

So church is not something you go to, but something you are part of. And an important part, at that!

Being a Christian is partly about what you believe, partly about how you behave and partly about being part of the faith community. It is about *believing, behaving* and *belonging* – though these three aspects are emphasised differently within different Christian traditions.

The idea of the Body of Christ with its many different parts makes clear that churches are not made up of clones. We are not all the same; we don't all believe or think the same way. Our likes, our concerns and our experiences are different; but we are all part of the same body. A phrase sometimes used is *unity in diversity*. But at times this seems an unattainable ideal. Many churches seem to attract 'people like us' rather than a wide range of people. Someone who is strikingly different may not be readily accepted.

Conflict and change

Churches cannot stand still. As society changes, so churches must adapt if they are to minister and witness effectively.*

Change always involves conflict, because different people have different views on every subject! Conflict is not wrong in itself; everything depends on the way it is handled.

As in any family, things can go wrong from time to time. Jesus himself addresses this question (see Matthew 5.23,24) and he stresses the need to do everything possible to heal divisions. Reconciliation, forgiveness and harmony are – or should be – vital ingredients of church life. But when all else fails, discipline is needed. This requires firm but sensitive leadership and is always painful. We shall return to this in Session 4 on 'Broken Relationships'.

A range of viewpoints

A few years ago, Professor John Hull delivered three lectures:

*A Church of England report which focuses on this is *Mission-shaped Church* (Church House Publishing, 2004)

- Can women and men read the same Bible?
- Can rich and poor read the same Bible?
- Can blind and sighted read the same Bible?

Behind these questions was an awareness that the Church tends to operate on the assumption that everybody understands things in much the same way. But do we? We bring our own varied backgrounds, experiences and expectations to church with us. Feminist, liberation, black and other theologies challenge some widespread assumptions about God, humanity and authority in the Church. We could develop John Hull's questions and ask whether black and white, young and old, able-bodied and disabled (or 'differently abled') can read the same Bible. This raises hard questions about who is included and excluded by the way we do things. We need to hear the voices of those who feel marginalised or excluded.

Abused children

The voices of those who have been abused are increasingly heard. At the end of 2002 *Churches Together in Britain and Ireland* published a report, 'Time for Action', which looked at the experience of survivors of abuse. It considered ways of making the church a safer place where people listen better. The report quotes William Crockett's words about the church as 'a people place'.

> *If this is not a place where tears are understood*
> *Where can I go to cry?*
>
> *If this is not a place where my spirit can take wing*
> *Where do I go to fly?*
>
> *If this is not a place where my questions can be asked*
> *Where do I go to seek?*
>
> *If this is not a place where my feelings can be heard*
> *Where do I go to speak?*
>
> *If this is not a place where you will accept me as I am*
> *Where can I go to be?*
>
> *If this is not a place where I can try to learn and grow*
> *Where do I just be me?*

It is tragic that some people have experienced church as a place where trust has been misplaced and abused; where their feelings cannot safely be expressed; where their experience is not heard; where conflict is not properly addressed. But their insights are, perhaps, leading to a new openness. Topics that were once unmentionable in many churches are now on the agenda. Could it be that the Holy Spirit is transforming churches into communities which are more open, honest, vulnerable and joyful?

QUESTIONS FOR GROUPS

SUGGESTED BIBLE READING: Romans 12.3-13

> Our faith became our best tool for becoming a happy family. Time and again we found something in it that illuminated a problem, clarified a puzzle or mended a hurt.
>
> *Sarah Johnson*

1. Raise any points from this booklet or the audio tape/CD with which you strongly agree or disagree.

2. How would Chloe and Tony be received in your church? On a five-point scale (1=poor; 5=excellent) how would you score:
   (a) the internal friendliness of your church
   (b) the welcome it gives to strangers?

3. In most churches, chairs/pews face the front. In others (e.g. Liverpool's Catholic Cathedral) people worship 'in the round'. What does the layout of your church building say about:
   (a) how God is perceived?
   (b) how Christians relate to each other and to the world?
   What changes (if any) would you like to introduce to the layout of your church building? Why?

4. 'Topics that were once unmentionable are now on the agenda.'
   (a) Compare church life today with when you first encountered it. Are you encouraged or discouraged?
   (b) Re-read the final paragraph of this chapter. Do you sense a new openness within your church and within the church at large?

5. Do you agree that three defining aspects of the Christian life are *believing, behaving* and *belonging?* Can you put these in order of importance? Would you add anything to or subtract anything from this trio?

6. The Church of England and Methodist Church have drawn up a formal covenant. Should we put time and effort into such schemes for church unity or is the quality of informal local unity what really matters? What helps relationships between Christians to grow and deepen?

7. (a) Which groups or individuals might feel excluded from, or marginalised by, your church? Why?
   (b) How would you distinguish between friendship and fellowship, or are they the same in your view?

8. List three aspects of your church life which you like most and three which you would change if you could. Share your ideas. (You might wish to consider local church life *and* broader denominational issues).

Closing meditation:

Read Colossians 3.15-17.

In silence pray for a few individuals in your church.

Then say the Grace together.

9. **Read Acts 15:36-41.** Describe recent changes in the life of your church. Did they bring conflict? If so, was this handled in a way which brought honour to the gospel? Should we aim to eradicate conflict from church life or are honest differences a sign of health and vitality?

10. **Read Ephesians 2:19-22** and **1 Peter 2:4-12.** List the various images of church in these passages. What other pictures can you think of? What does each image (e.g. living temple) say about the relationship between members? And what does it say about our relationship with Christ?

SESSION 3
RELATING TO STRANGERS

'You shall also love the stranger.' (Deuteronomy 10.19)

'I was a stranger and you welcomed me.'
(Matthew 25.35)

Bible times and modern times

It may seem strange in a course on relationships to spend a whole session thinking about strangers. After all, strangers – almost by definition – are people with whom we don't have a relationship!

Indeed, a common response to strangers is to mistrust them. Children are taught about 'stranger danger' (even though children are much more likely to be hurt or abused by people they already know). Asylum seekers receive a bad press and the assumption behind much that is written is that they are 'sponging' off our over-generous society. What is offered to them appears to be given very grudgingly. Some political parties seek to gain votes by exploiting distrust, suspicion and fear of people from different cultures and backgrounds.

A thread running through the Bible challenges this. In the words of a modern hymn, the people of Israel spent much of their early history as 'a travelling, wandering race'. When they settled in their own land they needed to be reminded of this history: 'You shall also love the stranger, for you were strangers in the land of Egypt' (Deuteronomy 10.19).

In this way the Scriptures invite us to use our imagination. 'Put yourself in the other person's sandals. Recall how your forebears felt when they were strangers,' urge the writers. The story of Sodom (Genesis 19), often used as a proof text in debates and arguments about human sexuality, is at least as much – if not more – a story about lack of hospitality to strangers.

Jesus the stranger

Jesus famously declared that 'the Son of Man has nowhere to lay his head' (Luke 9.58). He set out on his travels with his friends, always on the move, a constant stranger. And there was a sense in which Jesus' collection of disciples – and the bringing together of early converts to Christianity – was a gathering of strangers into a new family, a new household of faith.

In Luke 10.1-12, Jesus tells his disciples how to respond to the welcome (or otherwise) they receive when they move from place to place. The parable of the Good Samaritan suggests that our responsibility for others

> Every day 30,000 children die to utterly preventable causes such as hunger and disease. These are things we could change if ever we decided to.
>
> *Bishop Peter Price*

11

goes far beyond any narrow definition of 'neighbour'. Jesus' parable of the sheep and the goats (Matthew 25.31-46) makes it clear that welcome for the stranger will be one of the key criteria on Judgement Day.

A child who was told that he had an accent was amazed. Surely *he* was normal; it was the others who 'spoke funny'! Perhaps this tendency is inescapable? We strengthen our own sense of identity by comparing and contrasting ourselves with others. We want to feel superior to people 'over there' who are different. As we become more mature we are able to recognise difference as interesting and important rather than intimidating and inferior.

It could be that Paul's description of the Church as the Body of Christ (see Session 2) has a wider significance for society as a whole.

We actually *need* people to be different – to have different abilities, preferences and background experience – just as the body needs its different parts if it is to function properly. Seen in this way, diversity and difference can become something to celebrate in the rich experience of a multicultural society, rather than a source of division and tension.

Of course, this raises many difficult questions. Can people *really* live together and celebrate diversity, or are we always likely to prefer to mix with 'people like us'? We know that the worst extremes of intolerance have led to tribalism, civil war, ethnic cleansing, the Holocaust. We've seen all of these within living memory. But we've also seen signs of hope. South Africa is one obvious example, with Archbishop Desmond Tutu's 'rainbow people', and the Truth and Reconciliation Commissions. Recent developments in the Solomon Islands provide another encouraging example.

Our multifaith society

For many Christians, another challenge is how we should respond to other faiths. People of different faiths can live side by side in harmony but sometimes there is little tolerance. Each faith community can see itself as the exclusive repository of all truth. Sometimes intolerance explodes into violence. In contrast, in some communities, people of different faiths work closely together to improve mutual understanding and to build a more tolerant society.

Today we are more likely to use words like 'dialogue' than 'proselytism'. This presents a stimulating challenge to the great missionary religions: Buddhism, Islam, and Christianity. As Christians, are we in danger of soft-pedalling our evangelism? The great commission given by Jesus to his disciples was to preach the gospel to all. Are we at liberty to set that on one side in our multi-cultural society? Or can evangelism be gentle and sensitive as well as bold and imaginative?

Interestingly, there is evidence that leaders of other faith communities *welcome* straight talking and passionate enthusiasm by Christians about our faith, *providing*:

- we are willing to listen to *their* passionate enthusiasm
- we do not target vulnerable, impressionable individuals within their communities.

Strangers within the family

Sometimes, even our fellow Christians can seem like strangers. We seem to differ over a wide range of issues – from the services we use and the gender of our ministers, to whether the youth club should use the freshly painted church hall! Let's consider a few topical issues:

○ **Sexuality** – The world-wide Anglican Communion is in danger of splitting apart over the question of homosexuality. Some Christians believe that we should honour and accept life-long fidelity between couples, whether they are 'gay' or 'straight'. Others believe that so-called 'gay marriages' are an offence to God and cannot be tolerated within the church. Christians in Britain disagree strongly about these issues. There is also a significant geographical divide – with most churches in the South (Africa, Latin America, Asia) taking a more conservative approach.*

For some, all this raises the big question of 'truth or unity'? Should we suppress our strongly held convictions in order to maintain unity? Or is broken fellowship – always very sad – better than compromise?

○ **Young and old** – At a family service the Bible reader didn't turn up. At short notice a young teenager was asked to stand in and he read clearly and well. But where Bill went, his baseball cap went also. Without a moment's thought he read the lesson while wearing the (to some) offending article. Afterwards,

---

The Windsor Report 2004   published by the Anglican Communion Office addresses these issues

13

All the people in the world are like a big family, aren't they?

Mary Paterson (aged 6)

There are more slaves in the world today than there have been at any other time in history. The average slave in the American South cost £22,000 in today's money. Today, a slave (e.g. sweated labour, sex slaves) costs just a few pounds per week.

In the 2001 UK Census 70% stated their religion as Christian. Members of other world faiths amount to 6% (England) and 1.5% (Wales). Most are Muslims who naturally think it's 'better together' and live in cities. In a speech on 20 November 2004 the High Commissioner for Pakistan urged Muslims to integrate more closely into UK society.

some older folk complained to the vicar. You may be able to give examples of such tensions from your own church life!

○ **Social and political differences** – A few years ago I went on holiday with a Christian organisation. We were a very mixed bunch indeed: our group included people who were out of work and a district judge. It worked wonderfully well. Everyone happily used first names and related as equals. It occurred to me that this is unlikely to happen outside a church context and I was reminded of Paul's wonderful affirmation: 'There is neither Jew nor Greek, slave nor free, male nor female, for you are all one in Christ Jesus' (Galatians 3.28).

More recently I attended a service at which it was announced that a member of the congregation had been nominated as a prospective Conservative candidate for a seat in parliament. At the minister's invitation the man went forward. A small group gathered to pray for the politician, including a man who has served as a Labour councillor for many years. It was a moving moment.

Those far away

Before completing this session we must give some thought to relationships within our global community. Because of emergency appeals for the developing world, we sometimes assume that 'they' depend on 'us'. In fact, most of the dependence is the other way round. I eat a modest breakfast but each morning I am aware of my reliance upon farmers (probably poor women) in at least three countries, who produce oranges, nuts, tea and coffee. And of course every single European and American represents a far bigger threat to the world's diminishing natural resources than most people in the developing world.

We are becoming increasingly aware that our interdependence means we have responsibilities towards each other. These responsibilities may be reflected in our commitment to fair trade (*Traidcraft* etc), international debt remission (the *Jubilee* campaign, *Make Poverty History*) and aid programmes (*CAFOD, Christian Aid, Tearfund* ...). As the Bible makes clear, true relationships are two-way. There is giving and receiving. What this means – in detail and in depth – within a global context is of massive significance for the future of our planet.

QUESTIONS FOR GROUPS

> Over the years I have sung and lectured in just about every type of church you can name. Of the 195 churches I have visited, I was spoken to only once by someone other than the official 'greeter' – and that was to ask me to please move my feet.
>
> *Alison Gilchrist*

SUGGESTED BIBLE READINGS:
Deuteronomy 10.17-19 and Matthew 25.31-36

1. Raise any points from this booklet or the audio tape/CD with which you strongly agree or disagree.

2. Reflect together on your own experiences of being a stranger (e.g. first day at school; moving to a new town or village; starting a new job; travelling abroad; coming to a new church). How did it feel? What helped you feel more 'at home'?

3. Discuss the paragraph on sexuality (page 13).

4. Re-read and share your thoughts about the paragraph on Bill, the young Bible reader (pages 13-14).

5. Do you have encouraging (or discouraging) stories to share along the lines of the paragraph headed 'Social and political differences'? (page 14)

6. (a) Britain has always been a 'mongrel nation'. Should we welcome asylum seekers and refugees? If so, how? Or are they a danger to our stability, economy and racial identity?

   (b) Who are the strangers in your community? What is going on to help them feel more at home? What is your part in this?

7. (a) Do you have any views about the issues raised in the paragraph 'Those far away' (page 14)? In particular, do you agree that *we* depend on *them*?

   (b) Are you willing to pay more for goods carrying the Fair Trade logo?

8. It has been suggested that the fear of strangers which we instil into our children is counterproductive – needlessly leading to a nation of fearful children and parents. What do you think?

   Facts to ponder

   (a) Modern children are at no greater risk of abuse than children in earlier generations (speeding road vehicles is another matter).

   (b) If danger exists at all, it is more likely to come from family members or close friends than from strangers.

9. **Read Matthew 28.19-20.** Do you know people of other faiths? In your view should churches seek to work with other faith communities? Should we engage in evangelism among people of other faiths? If so, how should we set about it?

10. **Read Deuteronomy 10.17-19** and **Matthew 25.31-36.** What implications might this teaching have for you personally, for your church and for our nation?

Closing meditation:

Re-read the Bible verses at the top of page 11.

In silence, try to imagine what it must be like to be an unwanted refugee. Pray for homeless people in Britain and abroad then say together, 'Send us out in the power of your Holy Spirit. Amen.'

15

SESSION 4

BROKEN RELATIONSHIPS

Our quality of life is greatly enriched by good relationships, through which we are nurtured, cherished, encouraged, challenged and supported. In our closest relationships we find acceptance, trust and love. But, sadly, relationships sometimes go wrong and when they do, people can get badly hurt. They always have – see Genesis 4! —*Cain & Abel*

> *Be with us Lord,*
> *when in our experience*
> *light turns to darkness*
> *and the breaking of a relationship*
> *leaves us stunned in our soul*
> *and silent in our conversation,*
> *not knowing where to turn or who to turn to*
> *or whether life has a purpose any more. Amen.*
>
> (From *Vows and Partings*, Methodist Publishing House)

Broken relationships can be painful and deeply destructive. This is true whether we are thinking of relationships between friends or family members, or within or between communities, groups, or nations. Every day we see examples of this in the news: Israel/Palestine; Iraq; Sudan; Russia and Chechnya; Northern Ireland; resistance to asylum seekers; protests about land allocated to travellers.

From time to time things go wrong in all relationships, whether as a result of misunderstanding, intentional words or actions, or contrasting hopes, expectations and needs. Where there is commitment to the relationship, it is usually possible to overcome problems and to find healing and reconciliation. 'Conflict resolution' is one of the topics often considered in marriage preparation courses.

Forgiveness and reconciliation

Forgiveness, and the ability to forgive and be forgiven, is central to all this. It is a vital theme in Jesus' teaching. He is clear: our forgiveness must be without limit (Luke 17.4; Matthew 18.22). On a national scale, the Truth and Reconciliation Commissions in South Africa have demonstrated the healing power of such a process.

They also show that forgiveness is not easy. It means facing up to the reality of what we have done wrong, being sorry and saying so – the theological concept of repentance. It may involve attempting to make restitution. It will certainly mean trying to learn from the past and live differently in the future.

For the wronged person it may mean meeting the other person more than half way, like the father in Jesus'

> Forgiveness is the most important single word in conflict resolution ... [It] means searching for a new way, together.
>
> *Rabbi Jonathan Sacks*

16

story of the prodigal son (Luke 15.11-32). Giving – and receiving – forgiveness is often painful and difficult.

When things start to go wrong

'When you are offering your gift at the altar, if you remember that your brother or sister has something against you, leave your gift there before the altar and go; first be reconciled to your brother or sister, and then come and offer your gift' (Matthew 5.23-24).

When things begin to go wrong in relationships, it is usually wise to face the problem and attempt to deal with it. To deny or ignore difficulties and hope they will go away seldom works. Sometimes a third party can help people address the problems in their relationships. That lies behind the approach taken by *Relate* in its work with people experiencing difficulties in marriage or other personal relationships. Third party mediation is increasingly used as a way of handling disputes in the workplace or within communities – even in church settings.

Someone has to be willing to make the first move. 'It's no use building bridges unless you are prepared to cross them' (Archbishop Robin Eames, speaking about the situation in Northern Ireland). This is the justification used by those who have been willing to talk to terrorists. It was one reason for Tony Blair's historic meeting with Colonel Gaddafi in 2004. Such meetings bring criticism and condemnation as well as praise and understanding.

'Too broke to mend'?

Are some relationships 'too broke to mend'? This is certainly the assumption behind current divorce law in the UK, which speaks of 'irretrievable breakdown of marriage'. Previously, a divorce was granted if it was proved that a matrimonial wrong (adultery, cruelty, desertion) had been committed. The current law assumes that any of these wrongs can be forgiven and that relationships can be rebuilt. Proving these offences does not automatically lead to divorce. Divorce is granted only if it is shown that the marriage has irretrievably broken down.

Good in theory perhaps. But are the resources there to help people work through their difficulties at an early enough stage? Do churches have something to offer here?

For some Christians, divorce – and therefore remarriage – can never be an option. The promises made in a marriage service are for life. The commitment is 'for better, for worse'. The Roman Catholic Church takes a strict line on this – although it does allow some marriages to be annulled.

The Christian community is surely right to encourage couples to stay together and to offer all possible support. But does there come a time when it is necessary – perhaps preferable – to accept that a relationship has broken down? Should the victims of domestic violence be expected to continue to risk their life and safety – and that of their children?

When two people have gradually drifted apart and love has slowly died, is it better to acknowledge this than to live a pretence? But is this a pretence? Or is it the easy way – perhaps for just one of the partners?

When someone has been physically or sexually abused, it may never be right to expect them to face the person who has abused them. And when Christians encourage them to forgive their abuser, we may not realise the extreme difficulty of what we are asking. Some survivors of abuse feel that they have suffered twice – they have been abused and then made to feel guilty for not being able to forgive.

The fact remains that forgiveness is a central theme in the teaching of Jesus. Every time we say the Lord's Prayer, we commit ourselves to receiving God's forgiveness and forgiving those who hurt us. But it is a complex and incredibly demanding concept.

Perhaps we need to think afresh about what we mean by forgiveness. We are not required to think warm thoughts or to say kind words about those who have hurt us. Indeed, we may continue to experience hostile emotions for a very long time. True forgiveness requires us to avoid revenge and to act in their best interests, despite such feelings. Many who have – by God's grace – managed to practise forgiveness have testified to its healing power. Bitterness traps us in the past; forgiveness releases us into the future.

Towards healing

The Christian gospel says a great deal about the possibility of healing broken relationships - between people, and between people and God. Reconciliation is a recurring theme in the Bible, as is forgiveness. Experience shows that, with God's help, even after the worst breaches in relationships, people can move on and begin to find some kind of healing and forgiveness – even reconciliation.

QUESTIONS FOR GROUPS

> It is not the presence of conflict that is unhealthy for communal life, but the premature suppression of conflict in the interests of an inauthentic unity.
>
> *Nicholas Sagovsky*

SUGGESTED BIBLE READING:
Matthew 18.6-9, 15-22

1. Raise any points from this booklet or the audio tape/CD with which you strongly agree or disagree.

2. ⚔ A couple turn up at the church door after morning service. They explain that they were married in your church two years ago but now have major problems in their relationship. They are looking for help from the church that married them. The minister is on holiday. How would you/should you respond?

3. ✝ (a) A vicar who was attacked said that he forgave his assailants but hoped they would get a stiff prison sentence. Is this consistent?

   (b) Are Christians sometimes too quick to expect reconciliation when people have been badly hurt by the actions of others?

   (c) Should we forgive even if the person who hurt us doesn't repent?

4. (a) Do members of your group have personal experience of broken relationships and/or healed relationships, which they are willing to share?

   (b) Do members of the group have personal experience of struggling to receive and/or give forgiveness, which they are willing to share?

5. ✝(a) Restorative justice is now being used by courts around the world i.e. criminals are required to help or repay their victims. What do you think about this?

   (b) Do official apologies for sins committed long ago (e.g. the Crusades, the Inquisition, slavery, the Holocaust) have any real meaning or usefulness?

6. A woman discovered that her husband was abusing their daughters – an offence for which he was imprisoned. She forgave him and received him back into their home.

   Was that a wise/foolish/brave thing to do, in your opinion?

7. In a General Synod debate one speaker said that one in four women are affected by domestic violence at some point in their lives. She suggested that out of 60 women in a congregation of 100, 15 would be affected. This assumes that the church is an exact mirror of society at large. Do you accept this – or would you expect lower levels of violence and abuse within churches?

8. Four out of ten marriages in Britain end in divorce (or, put more positively, sixty per cent of marriages stay the course).

   (a) Does this have a positive side? i.e. are many people released from the misery of enforced togetherness experienced by many couples in earlier generations?

Closing meditation:

Ponder the words of Jesus, 'Forgive us our trespasses as we forgive ...'

In silence pray for those who have hurt you and those whom you have hurt. Then say together the Jesus Prayer of the Orthodox Church (see page 20).

19

'Lord Jesus Christ, Son of God, have mercy on me, a sinner. Amen.'

(b) Do couples give in too easily to pressures and stresses?

9. **Read Matthew 18.21,22**

'Bitterness locks us into the past; forgiveness releases us into the future'

(a) Is this statement true in your experience?

(b) Do you agree with the definitions of forgiveness on pages 16 (paragraphs 6 and 7) and 18 (paragraph 6)?

10. **Read Matthew 6.12** and **Luke 11.4**. 'Forgive us our trespasses as we forgive those who trespass against us'. What might this mean in practical terms for someone who has been:

(a) robbed? (b) deceived? (c) abused?

Rescued 'street children' from Colombia clearly enjoy being together

SESSION 5

OUR RELATIONSHIP WITH GOD

BETTER together?

A course on relationships in five parts

YORK COURSES

Written by David Gamble and John Young

Immortal, invisible, God only wise,
In light inaccessible hid from our eyes.

Words can never capture God. Often, our attempts to talk of God's greatness end up telling us more about what God isn't than what God is!

The well-known hymn tells us that God is not mortal, not visible and not accessible. God is separate and apart. God is holy. In the Old Testament, it was dangerous to come into God's presence. No one could see the face of God and live. We are wise to take off our shoes at the burning bush, for this is holy ground.

Yet that is not the whole story. There is another, much more intimate, thread in the Old Testament. Abraham was called 'the friend of God' (2 Chronicles 20.7). The New Testament emphasises this idea of the closeness of God (James 2.23). Matthew sees the coming of Jesus as a fulfilment of Isaiah 7.14, where the promised child will be called Emmanuel, 'God is with us'. However, we are not encouraged to get too 'chummy' with God. Like Aslan in the Narnia stories, there is more than a touch of wildness about the risen Christ. Jesus teaches us to love God, to trust God and to *fear* God.

Titles galore!

In a sense, it is extraordinary to claim that a human being can have a relationship with God, the Creator and Sustainer of all. Yet this claim is at the heart of a Christian understanding of faith.

In the Bible and over the centuries since, people have used many ways, words and images to describe God and their relationship with God. In his hymn *How sweet the name of Jesus sounds*, John Newton lists several titles for Jesus. In just one verse he uses ten! Each title suggests a very different – even contrasting – aspect of our relationship with Jesus.

Jesus! My Shepherd, Brother, Friend,
My Prophet, Priest, and King,
My Lord, my Life, my Way, my End,
Accept the praise I bring.

Father and mother?

God as parent, particularly father, is a popular image. It is a dominant theme in the teaching of Jesus. Jesus encouraged his disciples to think of God as 'your heavenly Father'. He even encourages us to call God 'Abba'. This Aramaic word is an intimate form of address. Our nearest translation is 'Daddy'. Yet some people with abusive fathers may find it hard to think of God in this way.

> 'God is friendship', said St Aelfred of Rievaulx. In our particular friendships, we catch a glimpse of what it means to be friends with God.
>
> *Peter Atkinson*

21

Some modern liturgies remind us that there are feminine images of God in the Bible. *The Methodist Worship Book* (page 204) opens a prayer with:

> *God our Father and Mother
> We give you thanks and praise ...*

It has to be said that this prayer caused some hostility. Why should this be? Hosea 11 and Isaiah 66.13 liken God's love to the love and care shown by a mother to her young child, as do the words of Jesus in Luke 13.34: 'How often have I desired to gather your children together as a hen gathers her brood under her wings?'

These images echo down the centuries. Anselm, Archbishop of Canterbury from 1093-1109, wrote, 'Jesus, as a mother you gather your people to you; you are gentle with us as a mother with her children.'*

Learning from human relationships

Different people develop their relationship with God in different ways.

Some spend time in a quiet place or a church. Others use visual images – pictures, candles, crosses, icons, statues. Regular prayer and Bible study; attendance at worship; sharing in Holy Communion; going on retreats; sending 'arrow prayers' throughout the day; 'chatting' to God; walking in the countryside; listening to music; talking with other people of faith ... there are so many ways of building and maintaining a relationship with God. Some people have pictures, texts, or symbols around the home as reminders that they are in the presence of God wherever they go. God is with them – bringing strength, encouragement and challenge.

It is also true that many people, even the greatest saints, find that God sometimes seems distant. Look through the psalms, where this is a recurring theme (e.g. Psalms 10 and 13). On the cross, Jesus quoted Psalm 22.1: 'My God, my God, why have you forsaken me?' (Mark 15.34).

How can we cope with these barren times? It is usually wise to confide in a friend and ask for their prayers and encouragement. The testimony of many is that even if we give up on God, God does not give up on us.

God as Three in One

In closing, we turn to the doctrine of the Trinity. Viewed in one way this suggests that God is great, holy and

*The Christian experience of God and the use of male/female terms when addressing God are discussed more fully in *Teach Yourself Christianity* by John Young (Hodder Paperback)

beyond our understanding. Viewed in another way, the notion of God as Trinity shows exactly the reverse.

The seeds of this doctrine are there in the New Testament. It was not devised by learned men in book-lined libraries. It came about as a result of the amazing experiences of the early disciples. They were Jews – monotheists – who believed that 'the Lord our God, the Lord is One'. Then they met Jesus. They knew that he was a real human being who got tired, hungry and thirsty. Yet after his resurrection they were forced to acknowledge him as 'my Lord and my God' (John 20.28).

Then came Pentecost. They were aware of a new power and energy within them. This surely was the promised Spirit of God? Yet they did not become polytheists who believed in three Gods. They continued to believe in *One* God – Father, Son and Holy Spirit. Their experiences tell us that the doctrine of the Trinity is practical and life-giving. It assures us that the God revealed in the Bible is:

- **The God who runs to us.** When the waiting father saw his prodigal son on the horizon, Jesus tells us that 'he ran' (Luke 15.20). Property-owning fathers in Jesus' day did not run. They were concerned to appear dignified and in control. This father threw all caution to the wind. In his delight he ran to meet his returning son. So with us. We have only to take one step towards God and he takes ten towards us. He longs for that deep, intimate parent-child relationship.

- **The God who died for us.** What is God like? This is no longer a huge, unanswerable, philosophical question. God in his grace has given us a practical answer. Look at Jesus. Listen to Jesus. When we do so, we find that God is tough on us – tough on indifference, tough on exploitation, tough on hypocrisy. We find, too, that God is infinitely gentle. He will not break the bruised reed, nor snuff out the smoking flax. He perseveres with us. He is the God who comes to save 'with healing in his wings'. That healing comes, not only from Jesus' teaching and example, but from his death on Calvary – and his resurrection from the dead.

- **The God who renews us.** We need forgiveness when we fail. And we need strength to get on with our lives as disciples of Jesus Christ. That strength comes to us from the Spirit of Jesus himself. God's Holy Spirit pours love and joy into our hearts and lives. These great gifts are not our private possessions. God wants them to overflow into our bruised and hurting world.

QUESTIONS FOR GROUPS

SUGGESTED BIBLE READING: Psalm 139.1-18

> The grace of our Lord Jesus Christ, and the love of God and the fellowship of the Holy Spirit. That is all, and that is everything.
>
> *Professor*
> *J. R. Watson*

1. Raise any points from this booklet or the audio tape/CD with which you strongly agree or disagree.

2. Flick through the pages of a hymn book and identify some of the words used to describe our relationship with God. What ideas do you find most helpful when describing your relationship with God? Why?

3. List a few of the points about human relationships you have discussed in previous sessions. How do these insights help as we consider our relationship with God?

4. A young mother starts attending your church. She wants to grow in faith and asks how your relationship with God started and how it has developed and deepened over the years. How would you answer?

5. She perseveres. How would you respond when she asks:
   (a) are you always aware of the presence of God?
   (b) how do you cope during times when God seems far away?
   (c) what do you find most difficult about your Christian faith and discipleship?
   (d) what aspects give you most joy?

6. At your annual church meeting a longstanding member objects to 'those new hymns and prayers which refer to God as Mother'. 'Our Lord taught us to say "Our Father in heaven", and that is good enough for me,' adds someone else. Describe the discussion which follows and give your own views.

7. Members of the group preparing for church membership are given the task of asking church members about their faith. How would you respond to a teenager who asks:
   (a) how you envisage God when you pray?
   (b) how you address God in prayer?
   (c) what advice you would give to someone who wants to learn how to pray?

8. Read the quotations from Archbishop Desmond Tutu and Harry Williams, an Anglican monk (page 22) and from Cardinal Basil Hume (box on page 23). Do you find them helpful/challenging? If so, in what ways?

9. **Search in St John's Gospel** for six titles used for Jesus. Take *two* of them and explain how they help you in your daily life.

10. **Read James 2.14-19.** On the tape/CD, John Bell asserts that the opposite of faith is not doubt but apathy. How might this challenge apply to you, your group and your church?

Closing meditation:

Discuss where you go from here. Outreach maybe? Disband, perhaps? Or further study – there are several more discussion courses available.

Read Desmond Tutu (page 22) then, in quietness, pray for fellow group members.

End the course by exchanging the peace.

'The peace of the Lord be always with you.'

'And also with you.'